SEX, CONS & ROCK 'N ROLL

A Tale of Love, Passion, and Betrayal!

Life can get Rocky. You have to roll with the Punches!

Gloria Moodie

 FriesenPress

Suite 300 - 990 Fort St
Victoria, BC, V8V 3K2
Canada

www.friesenpress.com

ISBN
978-1-5255-7534-1 (Hardcover)
978-1-5255-7535-8 (Paperback)
978-1-5255-7536-5 (eBook)

1. SELF-HELP, PERSONAL GROWTH

Distributed to the trade by The Ingram Book Company

SEX, CONS & ROCK 'N ROLL

.

DEDICATION

I dedicate this book to my wonderful son, who has brought me so much joy in my life. From the moment he was born, he has been my purpose.

I would not trade one moment with him for all the money in the world. He is my greatest achievement and has made me so proud.

I found this meme that perfectly describes our relationship.

"I will always need my son, no matter what age I am. He has made me laugh...made me proud...made me cry...hugged me tight...seen me fall...cheered me up, kept me strong, and at times driven me crazy. But my son is a promise that I will have a friend forever."

Disclaimer

Some of the things I say in this book regarding a person's race, religion, or culture are strictly my opinions and feelings, based on my experiences at that time.

They are not intended to offend anyone.

It is my experience that most people prefer to be in a serious relationship with someone that shares their beliefs, customs, traditions, etc. That is why there are dating sites specifically for Jewish people, or Christian people, or other special interest groups.

I am a mature, white, third-generation Canadian woman that has no religious beliefs, although I was raised Catholic. So my interests and experiences are mainly with men of a similar background.

I did not write this book to be politically correct.

In writing this book, I try to be as honest as I can be, so you can understand where I was coming from.

Again, I am not saying my opinion is right...I am just saying it is mine!

Note: Some of the character's names have been changed to protect their privacy.

PREFACE

I have been widowed, divorced, conned, lied to, and cheated on.

This book is often humorous, sometimes sad, but a mostly truthful account of my life and experiences; THE GOOD, THE BAD AND THE UGLY. I hope you laugh, and I hope you cry.

A big part of this book is the nasty truth about online dating and mature dating in general.

I will tell you about the bad guys, scammers, and con men, working hard to steal your money, the ones that make their living taking advantage of your vulnerability, by lying to you.

I will tell you how I was conned out of $10,000 by a man I thought loved me.

I will tell you about how I worked with the York Regional Police Fraud Squad to bring down one of these "*Romance Scams.*"

If you do nothing else, please follow this link to learn more about this:

https://www.youtube.com/watch?v=peb10yVpA2w
ps. I am "Joan."

I will offer you some real-life advice on how to navigate online dating, backed up with facts, as well as my experiences.

I will tell you the signs to watch out for, so you can beware of these fake profiles. I will tell you how to spot the men that are cheating on their wives or just trying to get in your panties.

I will tell you about the kinky fetishes out there; Doms, Subs, threesomes, sex clubs and more.

It is easy to say anything online and to present a false persona; people lie about everything; their age, weight, height, how much money they make, how they make a living, etc.

But there are also real people, genuinely looking for love and some real successes out there.

There will be people who read this and can relate to it; young or old, men or women, single, divorced, separated or widowed.

I will share with you some of the stories men have told me. It is not just us ladies that are lied to, scammed, and taken for a ride.

There will be people who will judge me; think me stupid, gullible or naive, shallow, and vain.

There will also be people who see the real me, a woman who started out insecure, just wanting to be loved, and how the journey has changed me.

Finally, I will show you how I found true love, the best kind of love.

Life takes guts.

It takes guts to move on after you lose your husband and have a young child to raise alone.

It takes guts to look for love again; to remarry and try to blend a family. Then it takes guts to move on when that fails.

It takes guts to go to dances alone, dinner alone, go to the driving range alone, and travel alone.

It takes guts to keep optimistic and cheerful every time you meet another cheater or liar and to keep putting yourself out there.

It took guts to write this book!

There are things I have done that I am not proud of, but I am proud of the person I have become!

ACKNOWLEDGMENTS

I want to thank the following people for their part in making this book possible. The people who have loved me and accepted me just the way I am.

To my group of friends from high school, thanks guys for being patient and putting up with me for almost 50 years.

To my large family (special note to my sister and father who have since passed), my thanks.

To *The Travelling Ladies*, we have shared so many laughs, tears, and adventures. You are my best friends and mostly my sisters.

Finally, to my late husband. My first love who I lost way too early, over 20 years ago. He was my best friend, and if given a chance, I would still be married to him.

Cover Art designed by a talented animator; Evan Sangster-Keeley

It All Begins and Ends with SEX

When I was a child, I loved the attention. I craved it. I wanted to be told I looked pretty. When we were little, mom always dressed us up for holidays and Sunday outings.

For Easter, we would wear dresses with ribbons and bows, a fancy bonnet, and shiny, patent leather shoes with a matching purse. Even my little brother had to endure a suit and tie, with all six of his sisters fussing over him.

When my older sisters were off doing teenage stuff, I was the leader. My younger siblings and I would play in the backyard, perform actually, for the neighbourhood kids.

We even charged them an admission fee to come and watch us. Usually, we played "witchy-poo" fashioned after a favourite television show of ours at the time.

With my long dark hair, slightly pointed nose, and high pitched screeches, I was the wicked witch. You should hear my cackle!

My late sister, two years younger than me, was usually my side-kick, while the younger ones were the kids I would torment.

Another favourite of ours was to play "snatch this pebble from my hand"…anyone recognize that one?

I loved to have my picture taken and be the centre of attention. I was quite vain.

But things changed as I came into my teen years. Going from a small grade school where you knew most of the kids to a big, high school with all kinds of kids you didn't know was quite intimidating.

This was when the confident little girl changed into an insecure young woman, unsure of how to fit in with the "cool" crowd.

I was fortunate enough to get a part-time job after school at a retail warehouse. I worked there from grade 10 through college.

Several girls from my high school also worked there, and over the years, we became the best of friends. We are still good friends after all these years, but back then, even with my friends, I felt inadequate.

You see, my parents split, then divorced while I was a young teen. Back then, that was unheard of, especially in my very white, middle-class neighbourhood.

Most of my girlfriends were dreaming of marriage and preparing their "hope chests," filling them with the things their mothers taught them were important. They were picking out their patterns for china, crystal, silver, and linens. They had been taught how to sew, cook, and bake.

My mother was gone. She left seven children with no mother to teach them the life skills that seemed so necessary at that time.

My father struggled to do his best, but with six daughters, he didn't have a clue what we needed.

I was also a bit of a late bloomer in terms of having the kind of figure the boys went after.

The popular girls were athletic, with long legs, well-developed boobs, and long (usually blonde) hair.

I, on the other hand, was short, a little plump, and was lucky if I could fill a 32A bra. No push up for me, nothing to push!

Back then, my best friends and I would go to dances and parties, looking for love. Most of my friends had boyfriends, but whoever was single would join me on the weekends trolling the bars and discos like the Generator, Misty's, or others that were so popular at the time.

I could tell you stories about the wild adventures my girlfriends and I shared during those years, but that would be another book.

This book is all about love, passion, and betrayal!

Sex. That's what boys wanted then, and that's what men want now. Well, most of them.

I met my husband a little later in life than most of my friends. While they got married, bought houses, and had babies, I was still searching for my guy.

Then, after years of being alone, going to parties and dances, trying so hard to find my Mr. Right, it finally happened.

I met this great guy; he was handsome, smart, and funny. He had a great sense of humor. He was a real jock, a hockey player!

We worked for the same company, both of us in sales. We met at the company Christmas party. He was so good looking and so much fun to be with. Everyone liked him.

He and I were great buddies. We had so many laughs. We went skiing, joined a bowling league, played volleyball, baseball, squash, and so much more.

He loved going to the cottage, and it was a big part of our life. We enjoyed ourselves so much together.

He was my best friend.

We did everything together when he wasn't out playing hockey and drinking beer with the boys.

But SEX was not one of those things. For whatever reason, romance and fun in bed were not one of our shared activities.

It was a challenge getting pregnant under those circumstances, but it did happen.

Mainly because I almost had an affair!

One night we had a party with his hockey buddies. There was this one guy. You know the kind...the one, all the women, find sexy, even though now I see sleazy, was a better description.

At the time, I thought he was hot. He had blonde hair and blue eyes. He was well built and was single. Most of the other guys had wives or serious girlfriends. This guy always showed up with someone new.

But that night, he was alone. Everyone was drinking, having a great time. Then all of a sudden, everyone was gone, including my husband.

While he had slipped away to bed, that guy was still sticking around. As the hostess, I was left alone with him, and one thing led to another...

No...we did not go all the way, but my husband did come downstairs and catch us with his hand down my top!

My husband did not get mad. He did not yell. He did not punch that dude out...even though he knew that guy was scum. Because he knew in his heart, he was not giving me what I needed. So things changed.

We decided it was time to have a baby. It took a few months of trying...and I mean TRYING!

My husband even insisted I stand on my head for half an hour while he went downstairs and had a beer. He tried to convince me this would make things *move in the right direction.*

Well, I was not that stupid, but what the heck, I really wanted a baby.

And that's how my son was conceived.

My son brought all the joy to my life that was missing.

My husband and I were both thrilled. I had never seen him so happy or proud as when he walked around with our little boy on his chest in his nifty little carrier.

Life was finally going the way we wanted. I had my little family. We bought a house and moved out of Toronto, got a boat, and even started to fool around again and then...

HE DIED.

One Door Closes and another One Opens

It had been six months since my love had died. At that time, I did nothing but watch my son and grieve.

I had quit my job to take care of my sick husband, but eventually, I knew I would have to work again. I would have to build a life again.

We had moved into our first real house in a growing city just about an hour north of Toronto. We had a small inheritance, and my husband had hoped for us to start a new life together, the three of us.

My dad and his second wife lived nearby, but the rest of my family were far away in Toronto. I had no friends nearby, again they all lived in the Toronto area.

I had no career, and there wasn't much in the way of prospects in my line of work without a commute to the big city. But my son was only eight years old at the time, and he needed me close by.

But ever the optimist, I decided it was time to get out and meet people.

My dad suggested I go to a PWP dance. He meant well, after all, that's where he met his second wife.

For those of you unfamiliar, that meant *"Parents without Partners."* My dad offered to babysit, so I got all dolled up...got my hair and nails done...bought a new dress...and headed out for an exciting night.

I walked into the dance hall, and there were about thirty people in the room; probably eight men and twenty-two women, or thereabout.

I was forty-one at the time, and everyone in the room except me was ancient. At least that's how it looked to me, although they were probably the age I am now.

The men were fat, bald, and reminded me of someone's grandpa...and the women they certainly didn't look like "Mrs. Wilson"...but close, but not nearly so sweet or kind.

I have never had so many eyes stare at me at once...and, not in a good way.

The men were licking their lips, while the women were shooting darts out of their eyes.

I bravely went and got a glass of wine, then asked the women if I could join them at their table. Their mouths said yes, but again...those eyes...if looks could kill!

No one talked to me...not one single woman.

The men looked me over while whispering amongst themselves. I was terrified one of them would come over and ask me to dance. I'm not sure what would have been worse...dancing with one of those old coots or sitting by myself all night.

So I did what anyone in my place would have done...I gulped my wine and ran home.

Once there, I cried my eyes out while drinking copious amounts of wine.

I thought my life was over.

I'm Worth Every Dime

After a few days of brooding and feeling sorry for myself, I did what I do best (no, not drinking more wine…LOL).

I made a life-altering decision. I was no longer going to be a mousy looking widow. I was going to reinvent myself.

I was going to become HOT!

I spent some of the money we had inherited; now, I had inherited!

The first step I took was to ditch the thick, plastic glasses I wore and the contact lenses I had battled with for years and had laser eye surgery. What a great feeling to be able to see clearly, without glasses. The boost to my confidence was immediate.

Secondly, I went and saw a medical professional...and for a few thousand bucks, I got the curves I always wanted.

While never exactly fat, I had put on a few "*baby*" pounds. A tummy tuck took care of that. Now I could wear tight jeans again and eventually, maybe a bikini. But that was not all I did.

Look out push up bras...I am now sporting a C cup!

Lacy bras in all kinds of colours now filled my lingerie drawer. I went on a shopping spree buying matching panties, bathing suits, and sexy tops.

Those young girls got nothing on me!

My final step in the new and improved me was to change my hair...from plain old brown to a sexy, fiery red!

Now I was ready to take on the world with all the confidence money could buy.

I took it Personal

Before digital dating and swiping images, there were the **Personals**. Not sure how many of you are old enough to remember it...this was way before cell phones, streaming, and social media.

Newspapers had a section at the back called the Classified ads where people would try to sell stuff. Just after the ads for real estate and cars for sale, they also had a little section where lonely people could place an ad looking for love. (Sometimes more than just love!)

You would read a short ad (what we now refer to as a profile), and if you were interested, you would call a number and leave a voice message with your contact info and some details about how fascinating you are.

There were no pictures to see...just words on newsprint and a voice on the phone.

My sexy new look was working...even if no one could see me. Confidence has a way of coming through.

Plus, I had years of experience in sales, so I knew how to sell. Soon I had messages in my inbox...guys calling me, wanting to meet me!

One of those guys was David. He was a little younger than me, and he was divorced. We chatted for a bit then decided to meet for a drink.

When he saw me...the look on his face...I knew I had spent my hard-earned money well and that the C cup was worth every penny.

We met at a bar for a glass of wine. I thought he was very good looking. He had a great body...nice abs and ass. I thought, "This was my lucky day."

Funny thing though...when he told me he had owned a restaurant I used to frequent with my late husband, and that he always greeted his guests...for the life of me I could not remember him.

Guess that was because I only had eyes for my guy!

But life goes on, and my guy was gone

So I saw him for about six months. He was not the love of my life. I was never going to marry him. But he made me feel good, alive again.

For the first time in a long time, I felt wanted, pretty, sexy, and desired. We had some laughs, and I had a glorious affair and tons of SEX for a time...until that grew tiresome.

I was missing intimacy, romance, and love, so I kept looking.

The personals kept sending me messages from new guys, and that worked for a while. Then one day, I met husband #2.

I honestly can't remember if Antonio contacted me, or if I contacted him, but he sounded nice, had a house, kids, was widowed like me, so I decided...what the heck...why not give him a try.

We met for coffee. Antonio was nice looking, very well dressed, and seemed like a gentleman. Our coffee date went so well that he asked me to go to a dance that night. I was thrilled!

My dad offered to babysit again...so off I went.

That night when he took me home, I asked him in for a nightcap. Well, one thing led to another...and no...we did not go all the way... but darn close!

That was the beginning of my first real romance and how I learned to enjoy the big "O."

The Big "O" and Chocolate Cake

I loved reading romance novels, especially the hot and steamy ones. I had never experienced the big "O" and had no idea what to expect.

I had made love before, and I had been f**d before, but according to these books, the big 'O' was sort of like climbing a mountain, and when you got to the top…there were fireworks! The ground moved, it even exploded…in a good sort of way.

Well, Antonio was pretty good at making the ground move, and the fireworks explode. In fact, he was so good they exploded all the time.

In the car, in the hot tub, pretty much anywhere. And for the most part…

I really liked it when they exploded.

But I soon learned it was not about me...it was about him and his ego.

Can you ever eat too much chocolate cake? Well, apparently you can.

Think of it this way...someone offers you a delicious piece of chocolate cake. It is rich, and it is creamy and oh so sweet. You savour it and eat every last morsel.

Then you are offered a second piece. You know you shouldn't...but you cannot resist. So you have another piece. It is still really, really good.

Then you are given the third piece. Before you know it, you are eating a 4th and a 5th piece.

It gets to the point where you don't want anymore. It is starting not to taste so good... you are full...and it has sort of ruined the taste of the first piece.

But sometimes it's easier to "pretend" you are enjoying it and get it over with.

Living with Little Italy

Italian Stallion, that's what Antonio thought of as a descriptor of himself. But that was far from the truth.

The only thing stallion sized was his ego. He wanted to drive a big ass truck, but he didn't want to shell out the big bucks, so he settled for a little SUV.

They say size doesn't matter, but husband #2 was not very tall, and he didn't have BIG feet if you know what I mean! Still, he did know what to do with what he had.

But I think our relationship was doomed for failure from the very beginning.

The first night my son and I had dinner at his house with his children; he surprised us. After a nice spaghetti dinner, he dropped the "V bomb" on my son and me.

Now, this won't bother a lot of you, but it sure as heck bothered us. He told us the meat sauce was made from venison, more accurately from deer meat.

My son broke into tears, and we both almost threw up on the spot, thinking how we had just consumed one of Bambi's relatives.

I do not like the idea of hunting at all. Especially not for sport.

I could never understand why anyone who has the money and the means to go into the grocery store and buy their dinner, would choose to pick up a weapon and kill an animal.

I could never get my head around going to Algonquin Park one weekend and taking pictures of the beautiful deer and moose we saw knowing that the very next weekend, Antonio was going up to the same area to see the same animals, but with a deadly intention.

I remember one day I was driving home from work and came across an older lady, her daughter, and grandbaby by the side of the road. They were visibly shaken and crying. I pulled over to see if I could help. They had hit a deer.

They had no cell phone, so I called 911 for them. When the officers came, they found the injured animal in the ditch and had to shoot it to put it out of its misery.

By then, I was crying as well. I called my husband to tell him why I was running late and you will never guess his response.

He actually had the nerve to ask me if there was any way I could get the poor, deceased animal's body in my car and bring it home for him.

I guess I should have known from that very moment what I was in for.

I know that different cultures have different ways of doing things. Antonio comes from a very traditional Italian background, and as hard as I tried, I just could not fit in.

What he wanted, what he needed, was a typical Italian wife. Like the one he lost. I am about as far from that as you can be.

His children, my stepchildren, spoke Italian. They went to a Catholic school where most of the students were Italian. The house we bought together was in an area with a lot of Italians.

When his parents were at our house, which was too often for my liking, everyone spoke Italian, except my son and me. It was like being a pariah in our own home!

They took over the kitchen, doing all the cooking, so we ate whatever they choose to make. Fortunately, I do love Italian food, and they were good cooks, so I guess it wasn't all bad.

However, the TV was also taken over by his parents, and of course, the shows they watched were in Italian.

His parents were invited, by him, to come over whenever they wanted, and of course, they stayed for days. I was never consulted, just told they were coming.

We quite often went to Italian picnics, and of course, everyone there was Italian. The food was Italian. The music was Italian.

My son and I hated it. But I tried so hard to be accepted, to be the good little wife.

Now don't get me wrong, I grew up in an Italian neighbourhood, and many of my friends over the years have been Italian.

My brother-in-law is Italian, and one of my closest friends' husband is Italian.

One of my favourite spots to travel to is Italy, and I love spaghetti!

But come on guys, I was only in my 40's back then, and spending my weekends with a bunch of OLD folks is not my idea of fun.

7

Well, That Didn't Work!

Both my parents were born in Canada. My mom's family is French Canadian and my dad's family came to Canada from Ukraine in the early 1900s.

That makes me a third-generation Canadian.

I come from a large family, and we used to spend a lot of our weekends playing various sports together.

At one time, we had a family golf tournament. Antonio happened to be on the winning team; therefore, in his mind, he is a good golfer. NOT!

I taught him how to play backgammon, a game my girlfriend and I used to play Sunday afternoons at one of our favourite watering holes.

So I was a reasonably good player. But he would not take advice or suggestions as to how to play better.

Backgammon is a game of luck or chance based on the roll you get. However, it is also an intellectual game, and winning is often the result of planning your moves, considering all the options before moving too quickly.

But as often happened, Antonio would get some lucky rolls that would result in his winning; therefore, he insisted that he was a better player than I.

The same goes for baseball, volleyball, or whatever sport we played.

My family is also very conservative in the way we dress. For instance, at a pool party, the ladies (even the slim ones) would wear a conservative one-piece suit, especially when we had a volleyball game planned.

The guys usually wore longer shorts that went almost to the knee. They were not tight in any way, shape, or form.

Well, we were playing one weekend, when my family was first getting to know my new husband. He came out of the house wearing a speedo suit, knowing full well we were going to play volleyball.

Every one of us, male and female, did not know where to look. We were so embarrassed. But his daughter said it best, when she shouted out **"Dad, we can see your package!"**

The vision of him playing volleyball in his speedo, cigar in one hand and a bottle of beer in the other, still haunts me today.

When we were first dating, we went to Wonderland theme park one day as a family. His children had recently lost their mother to an illness, as had my son lost his father. So all of the children were a little needing of motherly TLC.

The problem is there was only one of me. My son wanted to hold my hand, as did my stepdaughter. But my husband insisted that he hold my hand and told her to run along with her brother.

Then within earshot of her, he told me *"that I was the most important person in his life!"*

Well my answer back to him was

"My son is the most important person in my life, you may be one day, but not today!"

I remember one day he told his son to clean his room. He literally waited 15 minutes, and when his son had not yet left his game to come to do his chores, Antonio went up to his son's room and gathered all his clothes, books, sporting gear...whatever, and tossed them down the staircase.

Then he told his son, now you have a REAL mess to clean up.

I would not allow him to have any control over my son, so that was a major issue.

The way he raised his children was in a very controlling and manipulative way. There was not much I could do to help his kids, try as I might, but I could damm well protect my son from his overbearing personality.

One time we had this fight...I cannot remember all the details, but it was something about how much money he spent on me...all the gifts he bought me...my big three stone diamond engagement ring.

At first, he wanted to give me his late wife's engagement ring...a typical Italian style monstrosity that I would not be seen dead wearing. I told him he should give that to his daughter.

I wanted my own ring. I wanted a white gold solitaire. That was my style, simple, classy, elegant.

Well, he thought that I should have three stones. When he gave it to me, I thought, wow, he bought me a nicer, more expensive ring than I was expecting.

Until I learned about the "great deal" he got on it. You see, it was all about his ego, getting the biggest stone for the cheapest price.

Over the years, he did buy me quite a bit of jewelry, and most of it was very nice, as long as I got to pick it out.

But after another particularly loud fight, I stood at the top of our staircase and opened my jewelry box and sent every piece he ever gave me flying.

The children were shocked, and everyone ran around trying to pick up all the pieces. I told him, *"you may have paid for this jewelry, but*

Believe me; I have PAID for it, many times over."

I soon learned my value as a wife. When we would have arguments, he would say that he cooked our meals, he painted the walls, he mowed the lawn, shovelled the snow, and on and on.

Then he would say to me, "*what do you do*?"

I answered back, "I know your parent's anniversary and all your family's birthdays. I buy the gifts, cards and pick up the cake.

I send out the Christmas cards to your relatives and decorate the house.

I attend all the weddings and showers and buy (*and pay for*) a new dress and get my hair done for each, even though attending those functions is the very last thing I want to do!

I know the names of your children's friends and teachers. I know their phone numbers, where they live, and their parent's names.

I am the one who is there for your daughter when she has menstrual cramps or is crying over a boy, or trying to sneak out at night in a short skirt or top that is too tight. I am the one that said no to her piercing her nose.

I am the one that went on the roller coasters at Wonderland with both our boys because you were a *chicken shit*.

I got your son into soccer with my son and took him to the games you were too busy (*or lazy*) to attend. I bought and cleaned the equipment.

I picked your son up after work even though he made my new car smell change to that of French fry grease.

I am the one who plans time together with family and friends. And I could go on and on...but

I guess those skills don't add up to much in a marriage...not when being compared to fixing the dryer or cleaning the pool!"

8

Money Talked, So I Walked

When we were first dating, he was so romantic and generous. He was always taking me to nice places, lavishing me with gifts and wine. He would pay for our vacations. He even took me to our favourite restaurant and got down on his knee when he proposed.

He had a house in another city from me, closer to Toronto, so it made sense for us to move there.

However, I refused to move into his late wife's house. I insisted that if I had to sell my house and move, so did he.

His home was smaller than I thought suitable for a family of 5, and I hated the dark, heavy furnishings and décor.

You see he has twins, a boy and girl, and they were the same age as my son, so we had three 12 years old when we met, and they were about 14 when we married.

Together we made good money, so I convinced him we should buy a larger house and get a fresh start.

His kids did not have to change schools, it was just my son who had to make that sacrifice, but I thought I was giving my son the advantages of having a family and a father figure.

Everything changed once we married. Whatever we did as a family, the expense was paid out of our household account, whether it was ordering pizza, going to the movies, the arcade, or renting video games.

No longer was he paying for dinners out or my vacations …they came out of our household fund, which meant I was paying for myself.

I paid all personal expenses for my son and myself, such as clothing, but when it came to the house, I paid half of the property taxes, utilities, and maintenance.

At first, I didn't mind, as I thought I was in love, and the benefits would outweigh the expense.

Antonio made quite a bit more money than I did. A time came when I was no longer earning the kind of money that I was when we first started dating.

I could no longer afford the kind of lifestyle we were living. I could not pay my share of two vacations a year, weekends away, and dinners out.

I had sunk all my money into our home, but as he insisted that we not have a mortgage, I had no extra "*play*" money.

When I suggested we take out some of the equity in our home, he refused. When I suggested we change the ownership structure, to allow me some of *my equity*, he also refused.

Instead, he insisted that we sell our house, break up and go our own way.

I had one-third ownership, and he had two-thirds ownership, so I got one-third of the equity when we sold.

Never mind that I paid half the bills; for food, utilities, repairs, and maintenance, even half of our travel and dining out. That is when I realized how stupid I was to agree to that arrangement.

You see, we had signed a pre-nup, so what was his before our marriage would remain his, and what was mine would remain mine.

At the time, I wanted to be fair. It didn't occur to me that I had signed away my rights to his benefits or pension.

At the time, I thought I was so happy, and in love, I was thinking with my heart, not my head.

Now I am not saying he made all the mistakes. I made my share too.

Blending families from different cultures was very difficult. I tried very hard to be a good stepmother to his children.

It was a very stressful marriage with all kinds of hormones floating around; the kids all coming into their teenage years, I was starting peri-menopause, and yes, guys have menopause too.

I know I was drinking a bit more than I should have...I guess it's always been a de-stressor and a coping mechanism for me.

I realize now that I was unhappy, but I didn't know why. I should have been happy; I was married, and in love...or was I?

So, in conclusion, I learned that his Love for me was easy to give up. Money was more important than me.

9

Wash, Spin & Repeat

So now, you know I loved my first husband, and I *thought* I loved my second husband.

Now it's time to tell you about husband #3… well almost.

The personals were no longer an option, and I knew going to dances by myself wasn't the answer, so I decided to try this new phenomenon;

Online Dating, after all…this was 2008.

I was a little nervous, but I heard a lot of people were meeting and finding love with online dating. At the time, there were quite a few choices, EHarmony, Plenty of Fish, Match, Mate, OK Cupid; these are a few of the ones I remember.

Some of these dating sites were being advertised on television.

EHarmony had ads showing nice people finding other nice people for marriage, with a nice man telling you how they would help you find true love.

There were also some that sounded pretty seedy. I saw ads late at night that showed pretty young girls that somehow looked like they were selling sex...Is that legal?

There were sites geared for love and marriage; some were for certain religious groups, and others focused on age or interests.

I tried a few of them. I looked at other ladies' profiles, and thought, I am as pretty as them, or as smart, or as interesting...so this should be a breeze.

I wrote a compelling ad...I am, after all, a marketing grad.

In my profile, I gave details such as my age, weight, hair colour, etc. As well, I shared my interests and life goals. I put up a few pictures, although not a techy type, I did manage that ok.

Then I got my first "ping" that incoming mail sound you hear in the movies. I had messages!

Some of the men looked old...a lot of them seemed boring as hell, and some looked downright lecherous. Hmmm, maybe this is not such a good idea after all.

I did find a few men worth talking with. Some wanted to meet for coffee or a glass of wine.

I met several, but things did not go the way I had hoped.

Strangely enough, in person, a lot of them were not as good looking and did not look as young or athletic as their profile lead me to believe...

In fact, several looked quite different than their posted pics!

On the other hand, they told me I looked better...and I believed them...because they all seemed to want to see me again.

I later realized most of them just wanted to jump my bones.

After a few months of this, I got a "*ping*" from a guy named Andrew. He looked ok, although not handsome or sexy looking; still, he sounded like a nice guy, so I said yes to a glass of wine.

I met him at a restaurant, not that far from home. He was more interesting than I thought he would be.

He was a widower like me. He owned a construction company. He said he was romantic, wanted to travel, go wine tasting, enjoyed smooth jazz, slow dancing, holding hands...*our conversation flowed really well.*

I thought ...maybe this online stuff works after all.

He romanced me; he bought me gifts, flowers, and lingerie. He took me away for weekends, on a helicopter ride, took me dancing and to jazz festivals. We always held hands. I felt the old flutters returning to my damaged heart.

He had no children, so blending families would not be an issue. He was similar in age, race, and religion to me. He came from a very Canadian background, so I did not think there would be some of the problems I had with my second husband.

Most days, he came to my work and brought me a coffee. He met my friends and my family. I had not yet met any of his friends or family, but that was ok, I was happy again.

Things were moving very quickly. He was practically living with me. We talked about marriage; started looking at houses. He wanted to buy me a Cadillac.

Then he proposed!

I was ecstatic. We went to a jeweler I knew and looked at rings. I described what I wanted, and he was going to have it custom made. When he gave it to me, the stone was twice the size we had discussed.

Everything was going great.

It all started with him telling me about an investment he made that was doing so well. I thought to myself; maybe I should get in on this.

So I gave him some money to invest for me. Not a lot, a few thousand...

I could trust him...after all he was my fiancé

A few weeks later, he mentioned another investment, with the same result.

I gave him some money to invest for me. It was just a few thousand more.

Then one-day ...he didn't come home.

10

Smoke and Mirrors

I was worried. I could not reach him. I had tried his cell phone over and over.

We had plans that night. We were finally going to meet for drinks with some of his friends. It was now after 7 pm, and his friends were expecting us at 8.

Finally, I decided to call his partner in the construction company.

He was also worried; he had been unable to reach Andrew all day long. We decided he would check in with the hospitals, and I would call the police.

Well, I got a nasty surprise. A policeman came to my house. I told him all about Andrew missing. I told him about our engagement, even showed him my 2-carat ring.

Then he showed me the computer screen in his police car. He had pictures of Andrew, with different names and different looks, aliases, I guess.

It turns out Andrew was a professional con artist! A scammer. A convicted criminal.

And he was married to boot.

11

Dirty, Rotten Scoundrels

So the man I thought I was going to marry had lied to me about almost everything. He was married, not widowed. He was a professional con artist and a convicted felon.

When I spoke to his partner after the police left, I found out he was not a partner, but an employee, who had only been with this construction company for six weeks.

There were no investments.
My money was gone.

The police said there was nothing they could do about that as I gave him the money; the cheques were made out to him, not to an investment firm.

I lost close to $10,000,
plus my brand new laptop.

My beautiful, custom-designed, 2-carat engagement ring had to go back to the jewelers as the cheque he wrote when he purchased it bounced.

I told the police that he did that, not me, so why did I have to give back my ring. They told me that now that I knew the ring was purchased fraudulently, I must return it, or I would be charged with theft.

I was so afraid when I returned the ring that he would have swapped out the stone for a fake and that I would be held responsible, but fortunately, that must not have occurred to him.

Either that or he did not have the time to swap it.

Now I had to face the world, my family, friends, and co-workers and tell them what happened.

I was mortified with embarrassment and shame. I thought I was such a loser! Such an idiot, to have fallen for his lies. What kind of woman lets this happen to her?

I found out later that not all of it was lies, at least not totally.

Not that it's much consolation, but I think in his own way, he did have feelings for me. At least that's what his boss told me.

Apparently, he had shown his co-workers the ring days before he gave it to me, telling them how happy he was, and how much in love he was.

I think maybe he was conning himself as well as me.

12

A Man's Point of View

Somehow I managed to move on with my life. It helps that my son, my family, and my friends were so loving and supportive. They all knew what I had been through since losing my first husband.

I continued to meet men through various dating sites. I have probably tried every one of them out there.

I am a very outgoing and friendly sort, so I have no problem meeting with men. I have no problem initiating the conversation. Over the years, I have met quite a few men for coffee, drinks, or dinner.

I have probably met a hundred or so guys in the last 11 years. Some I have dated a few times, or for a few months. Some I am still friends with, and over the years, we continue to chat and share our experiences.

For whatever reason, things have not worked out romantically between us. But that is how I can share with you experiences *"from a man's point of view."*

There are a lot of nice men out there. Real guys, looking for the same things that most of us want. To be loved, to be accepted, to be desired. To have friendship, companionship, and yes, SEX.

I have had men tell me similar horror stories about women that contact them for sex. Women that are trying to steal their money in one way or another.

My son met his partner on one of these dating sites, and they have been together for almost ten years.

One of my closest friends from school passed away a few years ago, and her husband, now a widower, has also shared some of his thoughts and experiences with me.

I know from firsthand experience how hard it is to be a widow or a widower on these sites.

From my experience, widows are often the target of these "romance scam artists" as they prey on lonely and vulnerable women.

They often pretend to be widowers themselves to gain our trust and make us feel sorry for them.

Imagine the issues this causes for real widowers, good guys, who are truly looking for a new partner to love and share the rest of their lives with.

One fellow told me he talked to a lady (or so he thought at the time) for weeks. She sounded nice and reasonably interesting, so he asked her out for a coffee. In the pictures she had on her profile, she looked attractive.

When he got to the restaurant, he looked around but could not find her. This woman approached him, and in his words…

"she was fat, her hair was dirty and greasy, and she had food stains on her sweatshirt." She laughed when she saw the look of horror on his face.

She said something to the effect of *'guess I'm not exactly what you were expecting, but now that you are here, you can buy me dinner.'*

In return, he pulled out a $20 bill and gave it to her and told her she could buy her own dinner. Then he left.

I told him he was silly to have given her the $20. If it were me, I would have turned around and left her on the spot!

Many men have told me that they have met women in a similar situation; mostly, the women do not look like their profile pictures. They are heavier, or older, or slutty looking, or they look like someone's grandmother.

Men also get women that are looking to be taken care of financially. Women that expect expensive dinners out, gifts and vacations away.

Women that are basically selling sex in return for cash or compensation by other means.

Here are some screenshots of conversations with men that have told me part of their experiences:

I got too many female scammers with fake pics, fake locations and fake profiles do not only men who are scammers. The last one was discovered yesterday when she told me before that she was a cancer patient form out of town and she wants to come and see me when she visits her doctor's' appointments. Few days later she wrote saying that she was scammed with 42 00 dollars and she needs my help.Lol.....lol...you can not beat this crap.... Lol. I am not looking to be a volunteer in any dating site. If I volunteer I do in my community so I did not even reply to her weird suggestion to come and visit me .Although I did not reply, she still went with her scam. Thank God we all have the lovely BLOCK button. Cheers. Oops...I am Bill.

uwantacoffee

I want to be in your book................Just as many women that are dishonest on this site

lovespinot

i totally agree
send me an email lovespinotgloriam@gmail.com

uwantacoffee

I have been asked for money for sex and sex for money on this site and some women are not in Canada..........LOL

Lots of men have told me that after chatting for a while, they get the story "*I just need some money to pay for my car to get fixed*" or "*my child is sick and needs an operation*" or some such bull.

So YES, men get lied to, cheated on, and conned as well.

13

I Seem Normal, Right?

At this point in the book, I want you to see how I advertised myself; what I was looking for.

You see, my profile shows a real woman, not young, not slim. It shows my wrinkles and weight. A woman not beautiful to all eyes, but feminine, well-groomed and attractive nonetheless.

I clearly state what I am looking for…a long term relationship with a partner to share and enjoy life with.

My profile outlines my interests and hobbies, such as travel, wine, reading, writing, business, family, golf, backgammon. I state my real age and occupation. I should come across as intelligent, ambitious, successful, and fun.

Nowhere in my profile does it say, "I want to get laid…or that I am here just for sex."

My profile clearly outlines that I am looking for a man in a similar situation, with similar attributes and interests.

So why do I get 30-year-olds pretending to be 60? Why do I get the sexual messages like *"hey baby wanna have a threesome?"* or *"you look good enough to eat."*

I especially do not want to *show you mine... or see a pic of yours.*

Is there something written on my forehead that I don't see? Is there a scarlett letter?

Yes, there is the boob shot...and some of you will say...well, that's what you advertised.

And you are right, but I have tried just showing pictures of my pretty face, and describing how smart and interesting I am...and came up empty-handed.

Men are visual. To get a man's attention, any man, I needed to sell myself. And boobs do it.

This is my Plenty of Fish Profile, as well I have one like this on many other dating sites.

lovespinot : backgammon or golf, who's up for a challenge

Highlight Now

About	Non-Smoker with Average body type	City	Toronto, Ontario
Details	62 year old Female, 5' 1" (155cm), Non-religious	Ethnicity	Caucasian, Aries
Intent	lovespinot is looking for a relationship	Education	Some college
Personality	Hopeless Romantic	Profession	Marketing Manager

Interests

Wine	Business	Pool
Travel	Golf	Cooking
Music	Bowling	Boating
Reading	Backgammon	Anything on or by the water
Family		

About Me

Smart and sexy lady looking for romance, adventure and someone to enjoy life with...I am easy going and fun to be with, adventurous and playful...flirty, witty and competitive...up for many challenges... yet interesting and intelligent...feminine yet tough. Successful and ambitious, family oriented and very independent...but wanting to share life's adventures...in other words a great catch!

Looking for a man that can keep my interest. Like me he is a successful, intelligent, confident, handsome, sexy, romantic man not afraid to go after what he wants. Like a man that appreciates wine , travel, business and intelligent conversation.

But yet despite a great profile, I kept getting the wrong kind of guys...including the ones that lie about their age and that are only interested in SEX!

TomJones99

Hello Lovespinot, my real age is 41 but I liked your profile so much I used this method to contact you as PoF cuts me off at a certain age to talk to people.

lovespinot

I understand

But you are way too young to be of interest to me

TomJones99

No, I'm not:)

lovespinot

I am 62

You are 21 years younger than me

What could we possibly have in common

TomJones99

Who knows, we can always find out

misterplsandthnku

Well hello there!

How are you doing this afternoon Ms. Pinot?

I'm sure this isn't the first time you've been approached by a younger man (I'm 36, not 52) and I really hope that something about my message will at the very least put a smile on your face. A reply would be even better...

I know that the odds aren't in my favour, but I had to take a chance and say hello after stumbling across your profile. Do you think you could get along with a cute and mature younger man under the right circumstances maybe?

I'm looking forward to hearing back from you hopefully...

lovespinot
How old, or should I say, young are you?

alled4321
LOL...guess ?

alled4321
i'm 35 but attracted to older mature lady like you.. do you like younger guys? ever dated my age?

mmssttk0009
Do you like younger guys?

lovespinot
Did you see my new profile

mmssttk0009
Yes but I am 30 and curious

I am not on this, or any dating site, to satisfy someone else's curiosity. I am not here to teach a young guy how to get laid.

I am here looking for love, for a real relationship and for someone to grow old with.
And then there are the dicks...quite literally

Jacobfee
Maybe I shouldn't have sent the email...

lovespinot
I deleted it

Jacobfee
So you didn't like it.

lovespinot
I don't like pictures of dicks
I never asked for it
And I'm tired of all this sex stuff

I remember getting an email once and opening it up at work only to see a picture of a very large and hard...you know what.

But truth be told, I would rather have a man come right out with what he wants. I can then decide if I want that tonight, or tomorrow, or ever.

What really burns my butt are the men that lie, cheat, and try to CON you.

14

Speaking of Sending Pics

I had been seeing this guy for several months. We had been intimate. So he had certainly seen my "*girls*." But like a lot of guys, he asked me to send him some pictures.

I hate taking selfies. It is hard to take a good selfie of yourself that is sexy. But he was my boyfriend, so I thought, what the heck? How can it hurt?

So I opened up my razor cell phone, a cute little flip job (that was the style back then), and snapped a few shots. I found his email address, and with the press of a button, I sent him my steamy shot. A minute or two later, I got a responding email. But it wasn't from him.

The message said, "Mom! Did you just send me a picture of your boobs?"

With horror, I realized I had somehow sent this picture to my son. I don't for the life of me know how that happened.

When I checked my sent file, the email was addressed to my boyfriend, not my son.

Then I thought, "Oh my god! What if it went to all my contacts!"

I have a tattoo of a butterfly on my upper breast, so even though I was smart enough to take a picture that did not show my face, my son recognized me.

I answered back..."*well, I sent someone that picture. But I did not send it to you. I sent it to the guy I am seeing.*"

My son was in his early 20's at the time, and boy did he give me a lecture!

He told me I should never send pictures like that over the internet. You never know who might see them, he said.

He told me what if my boyfriend shared that picture or posted it somewhere. What if people you knew saw it?

My son, of course, was right. I should never have done that. I have never done that again.

But a really strange thing happened next... after my lecture I closed my flip phone and put it down.

All of a sudden, the phone started making noises...click...click...click. It was taking pictures, with the lid closed.

My phone never worked after that day. I don't know what happened, but

I guess my boobs broke my phone!

15

Dating Disasters

After almost eleven years of online dating, there are so many stories to tell, but I will limit it to a few; to give you some idea of what it's like out there, and to give you a laugh.

I can't count how many men I have dated that I think were married, or at least in a relationship.

One of my first experiences was with Neil. We talked on the dating site for a few weeks and then decided to meet for a drink at an upscale Italian restaurant.

He was very handsome and sophisticated looking. He wore a nice suit, as we were meeting after work. He told me he worked in the financial industry and was Vice President of Sales for a large company.

We had a few glasses of a very good wine, and then he walked me out to my car. He asked if he could see me again, then leaned in for a kiss. It was nice. Very nice. I got that happy, giddy feeling again.

The next week Neil asked me out for dinner. He wore a suit again as it was a Tuesday night. He held my chair out for me and helped me with my coat. Then he told me how pretty I looked.

He ordered us a very expensive bottle of Cabernet Sauvignon, one of my favourites. We talked about wine for a while, as I am a bit of a wine enthusiast. We talked about business and travel, more of my favourite conversation topics.

After dinner, I invited him back to my place, where we had some more wine, and played some backgammon.

I really enjoyed the evening, so I was excited when he gave me a few more kisses, followed by asking if he could see me again the next week.

This went on for three or four weeks; dinner, drinks, backgammon...

Neil was very attentive and complimentary. I was feeling quite good about things, but I did wonder why he was only taking me out during the week. So I broached the subject.

He told me he was going to the cottage the following weekend with his children. Ok. That was reasonable. Next time I asked him, he told me he would be out of town on business, and that would extend to the weekend.

Ok again. Reasonable.

But, there was something niggling in the back of my brain. So I decided to call him. He had given me his cell number, but every time I called, it went to voice mail. I would leave a message, and he would get back to me awhile later. It all seemed reasonable.

Until it didn't.

One time after trying to reach him for a few days, I decided to look up his work number. He had mentioned the company he worked for, as well as his title and his last name. So I called the number and asked the receptionist for his extension.

He did work for that company, and that was his last name, but that was not his title.

I then googled him and found his Facebook profile, with a picture of his wife and kids. When I called him on it...I never heard from him again.

Guess I've been ghosted!

There have been several guys I have dated for two or three weeks, or months, with the same kind of conclusion. After a while, even a dummy like me gets the picture.

Well, another one bites the dust.

Some men (and women) use older pictures of themselves when they were younger, slimmer, or had hair!

Some list themselves as having an average or athletic build, when that is far from the truth.

There are various lies, big or little, intended or not.

Another guy I met insisted on taking me out for dinner for our first meeting. I suggested we get a coffee or a drink, but he kept saying he wanted to take me to dinner. So I relented and said yes.

He asked me to meet him at a Swiss Chalet near where he lived. I was not thrilled to have to drive the half-hour, and even though I like Swiss Chalet, it is not my idea of a date location, but again, what the heck.

When he walked into the restaurant, he was at least 100 lbs. heavier than his picture. I'm sure he could tell by the look on my face that I was surprised and disappointed.

Why do people do that to themselves? Why do they set themselves up for pain and sorrow?

So we sat down and ordered dinner. To my way of thinking, I would have expected him to say something like, "*I just joined a gym*" or "*I just started a new diet.*" Anything that would at least give the impression he knew his weight was an issue and was working on it.

He did just the opposite. All he talked about was food…how he loved this or that smothered in butter or sauce, etc. Do you get the picture?

But this guy did not wait until after our meal to ask the "*Awkward Question.*" No, I got it with a fork full of chicken halfway to my mouth! "*So, are you going to see me again?*"

I politely answered that I did not think so. He then said, *"I figured that. So are you going to pay your half of the bill?"* I pulled out a $20, laid it on the table, and then

I got up and walked out in the middle of our meal.

We all have our personal preferences. What qualities we are and are not attracted to, physically but also intellectually, culturally, etc.

For myself, I prefer to date men that have a similar background to me; a similar upbringing, family values, the kinds of food we eat, the holidays we celebrate, and so forth.

So for me, this means white guys, that are pretty much WASP. (White Anglo-Saxon Protestant)

I am also really picky about accents. Some I like, such as English, but Eastern European, or most European, do not appeal to me, especially if they sound like they just got off the boat if you get my meaning.

So generally, I have no interest in dating men that are quite different in my mind, such as African-Americans, Asians, Indian's, Jews, Muslims, and other religious men (myself not being religious at all).

What can I say…that's just me!

So one day I met a man for a drink. He did not have his picture on the dating site. Some people don't like to post their image as they do not want to be seen by people that may know them or work with them.

That is understandable. However, he had emailed me his image at my request.

When I saw it, he had a ball cap on, and it sat low on his face obscuring it a bit. But he looked in reasonably good shape and seemed ok.

I met him at a restaurant, and he had that same cap on, but when he looked up at me, it was clear he was Asian.

I was a bit surprised, for some reason I had not noted that on his profile, but that's ok…we could still have a drink and talk.

The conversation was fine, as I am quite experienced at talking with almost anyone from my years in various sales positions.

But as our drink ended, I thanked him and said I had to get going.

I think that men should have a sense of how a woman is feeling during a conversation, her interest level.

I was being nice and chatting away, but I was not my usual flirtatious self. When I am interested in a man, he should certainly pick up the clues.

However, when I am not interested, he should also see the signs. But apparently, he did not.

So he walked me to my car, then came that awkward moment when he asked me if he could see me again.

I hate being put on the spot like that. I much prefer to get or to send a text so you can let someone down gently.

But I don't like to lie, and I don't like to hurt someone or be rude, so I told him I didn't think so.

Instead of taking it well, *he got mad at me*. He asked me why, and I explained to him that his profile image was unclear that he was Asian, and that I prefer to date white guys.

That is when he said to me, "*I should bend you over your car and FUCK YOUR BRAINS OUT.*" My response to him was

"Someone can bend me over my car and FUCK MY BRAINS OUT, BUT IT WON'T BE YOU!"

One of the strangest days I had, however, was a day I had two dates, both disastrous.

In the morning, I was talking to a gentleman. He invited me out for a coffee. I met him at Timmy's, a local coffee shop. When I got there, he was already seated and drinking. He did not get up to buy me anything, so I got in line, got myself a tea, and joined him.

He asked me a lot of questions, much like a job interview.

I was not liking this much.

So far, he had shown me he was not a gentleman, and asked questions that were pretty personal. I discovered during our conversation that he was Jewish.

What came next was the killer.

He leaned back in his chair and looked me over, much the way you would look at a tank full of lobsters while you were deciding which one you wanted to eat. Then he said those profound words,

"I would have sex with you!"

Wow. Can you believe it? I guess I should be thankful that he would have sex with me...like no one else was willing to take on that monumental chore. I could not believe my ears.

If that happened to me today, instead of back then when I was inexperienced and insecure,

I would have gladly given up my steaming hot cup of tea to pour it over the jerk's head.

But this day was not over yet. Later that day, I had an even more disastrous date if you can believe it.

After a few hours of going back and forth between crying and feeling sorry for myself and getting so angry that steam was coming out of my ears, I went back on the dating site.

I am nothing if not resilient.

So another guy gets chatting with me. Again, he sounded and looked nice. This time the invite was for a drink. By this time, my ego needed a boost, and a drink or two sounded in order.

I got dolled up, quite sexy looking, as I said my ego needed the confidence boost.

I walked in and sat at the bar as we had agreed. In came a man that was a bit swarthy looking.

Uh oh! Not what I was expecting!

He sat down and looked me over. He asked what I wanted to drink, and I ordered a glass of Pinot Grigio, one of my usual go-to drinks, and I could tell I was going to need the big glass!

We talked a bit, but truthfully he was not looking at me much at all. I wondered why he was even there. I do look like the pictures I posted, so he must have liked my looks?

As it turns out, he was Muslim.

Now I have nothing against Jewish or Muslim people. Truthfully, I don't know much about them, but I get the impression they are pretty different than what I am used to.

If these two men were any example, they could not have been less my kind of guy. They were obviously the kind of men that feel women are below them and are there to serve them and their needs.

I guess I was suitable to have sex with them, but not good enough for intelligent conversation. Heaven forbid, I actually had thoughts, opinions, and control over my own destiny.

But there still was something to come… something that made that day even worse!

While at the bar, gulping my large glass of wine and wondering how quickly I could make my exit, in walked a very good looking young man!

He had his back to me, but there was something familiar about him, the way he moved.

He sat down at the bar, not facing towards me, then I heard his voice as he ordered a beer.

Finally, he turned around, and I got a good look at his face. And he got a good look at mine.

It was my stepson! He looked at me, then at my date, and I knew that soon my ex would hear of

my dating disaster!

16

The Language...not of Love!

One of the things you learn or need to learn, as you age and become part of the modern dating world, is the new slang or dating lingo.

Texting, tweeting, and dating sites all have their own language, and it is not necessarily the language of love.

Most of us are familiar with OMG, LOL, and LMAO...

Then there are words or terms like FWB, getting an emergency call, getting curved, cushioning, breadcrumbing, BDE, being catfished, and being ghosted, just to name a few.

FWB stands for friends with benefits, which has been around for a while. This is a somewhat classy way of referring to two people that consider themselves friends but are having a casual, sexual relationship.

They generally are not a romantic couple but are just having a good time together, which includes hanging out, and doing things, with both usually splitting the bill.

While some guys are looking for a **F*ckBuddy** and just want to hook up. Many guys say they want a long-term relationship, when in fact they are actually looking for either FWB or the other!

Getting an **Emergency Call** should be pretty obvious. It is a planned way of getting out of a bad date. Before you meet that someone new, you make an arrangement with a friend to call you while you are on the date.

If it is not going well, you pretend they called due to some emergency...like your brother just got hit by a MACK truck, and you have to rush to the hospital.

Some of these excuses can be so ridiculous that the person you are lying to can see right through the hoax. However, some of the recipients are so dense that the tale becomes believable.

I have, in fact used this ruse on occasion if I am somewhat concerned about my level of interest I have or a concern for my wellbeing and my bones being jumped.

It has saved me from bad judgment calls at least a time or two!

Getting **curved** is a polite way of saying rejected or turned down. Sometimes it is a big, fat NO! Like when you send a cute guy a witty message, and he blocks you, while other times it is just a quiet, no response, leaving you wondering if you just got CURVED.

But sometimes you are being **cushioned,** which means you are being led on, or used, as a backup plan, no doubt one of many being strung along. In the old days, this was called "playing the field."

Yet other times, you may have been **breadcrumbed**, meaning that the guy you have been chatting with for a period of time has been sending you flirty, but non-committal messages.

In other words, the chicken shit is afraid of confrontation and doesn't have the guts to tell you he is really not that interested.

BDE or Big Dick Energy refers to that guy that exudes so much confidence he does not need to be loud and brag about himself. This is a really hot guy!

I like to think I have BDE, or at least will someday!

Being **catfished** is one of the major topics of this book, unfortunately for me. When someone you are talking to does not feel real, when they have excuse after excuse why they cannot meet up, when they say things that conflict with something else they have said, you may be being catfished.

For example, a guy says his child is 12 then later says they are 16, or he says he is an engineer but later says he is an architect.

This can be as innocent as someone lying about their age or weight, or it can be a real attempt to lead you to believe they are someone they are not, such as rich, or even single.

This can be a con artist such as that jerk I thought I was engaged to, or as some others, I am yet to tell you about.

Finally, for this chapter, there is **ghosting**. This is another thing I have experienced time after time. This is when things seem to be going really well.

It can be just chatting online for weeks with you believing you will eventually meet, or you may actually be dating and feel that things are becoming more serious...then suddenly, out of the blue the recipient of your affection

...disappears into thin air...just like a ghost!

17

Kinky Stuff

I had no idea there were so many kinds of kink. I did not even know what a fetish was or that I was considered *vanilla*!

My ex had a thing for stockings with heels and garter belts. That was not too weird. Lots of guys like sexy lingerie. Right?

I thought it a little strange that he preferred when I had worn the stockings a few times, and they had a bit of stinky feet smell, but apparently, that is part of having a foot fetish...the good part meant lots of foot massages!

The not so good part about fetishes was he occasionally liked to give me a spanking. Now I don't mind the odd playful, smack on the butt, but spanking was not my idea of a fun time.

Partly because it was painful when he did it too hard, but mostly because he was stronger than me, so it was his way of controlling me.

I do not like to be controlled. I did not like to be spanked!

Over the years, I have met quite a few guys that had some sort of fetish.

Another guy I met once asked to see my feet. When I took off my shoes, he got pretty excited and told me I had *FRED FLINSTONE TOES*...that is not something a girl wants to hear! *Wilma* toes maybe, but not *FRED*.

Lots of people, men, and women get turned on by role-playing and fulfilling a fantasy, such as being tied up.

Most of you will be familiar to some degree with the book and movie "*50 Shades of Grey.*"

This is where I learned a bit more about the whole Dom and Sub fetish; the roles and bondage rituals.

Usually, we think of it as the man dominating the woman, but sometimes you see the woman dressed in black leather and heels with her handy, dandy little whip!

I have to admit there are a few men I would like to whip, and this has nothing to do with sexual pleasure!

Many men on these dating sites get aroused by one or more of these fetishes to some degree. Some come right out and tell you, or have it in their profiles, while some don't let on until you have dated for a time.

I talked with John for a month or so when he told me about his kink. It is called *Financial Domination*.

He wanted me to demand his wallet; he wanted me to tell him how much money he should have in his wallet each and every time. (His suggestion was to start with a thousand and work my way up).

He wanted me to demand his wallet and take out the money every time I saw him.

If there was not sufficient in there, he wanted to be punished.

I will admit to being a little curious, so I asked him questions about it, rather than just blocking him off the site, but for the life of me I could not understand it, so we never did end up meeting.

Lots of men are very nice and could be great husbands or dads or partners if you can accept their secret desires.

It is actually quite common for men, especially successful ones, to want to be controlled by a woman and take the submissive role.

They may be powerhouses in the business world, but when they get home, they want the woman to take charge.

In many cases, this is not just about sex but something they want in a regular relationship.

Some fetishes, though, are just too hard to understand.

Did you know that there are places in most major cities that are *SEX CLUBS*?

I did not know that until my con artist fiancé took me to one. It was in the suburbs of Toronto. I thought it was a regular bar.

We paid an admission fee and had a drink. I noticed a lot of women were dressed extremely sexy…wearing see-through blouses with no bra or tops showing lots of cleavage, etc.

When we got up to dance, I saw a man getting a blow job in the corner. OMG.

Then I felt a hand on my ass, and it wasn't my fiancés'. In horror, I told him, "*a man just grabbed my ass,*" but he thought it was pretty funny.

Then he told me what kind of place it was. He told me there was an area in the back where we could go...he said there were rooms you could use to have sex with other people watching, or you could watch...or join in with a group... threesomes or more.

I could not believe this was not against the law!

I told him I wanted to leave, so we did. I was pretty upset. He told me that these places were much more common than I knew. He wanted to go back again sometime, but I refused.

Then another man told me he wanted to be a cuckold. I had no idea what this was. He explained to me it usually occurs between a man and his wife, but in our case, he would make an exception.

He wanted me to have sex with other men while he watched, therefore humiliating him.

OMG...that one did get blocked!

I'm not a prude. I have been around the block more than one time. I don't like to judge people; to each his own. Some things are fun to try in a safe and comfortable relationship.

Sometimes a marriage or relationship needs to spice things up a bit. As long as people are consenting adults, what they choose to do is not my business.

What I choose to do, or not do, is my business!

I always liked chocolate, but now I think I prefer vanilla.

18

Fool me Once, Shame on You

During the eleven or so years, I have been on various dating sites I have talked to a lot of men I suspect of lying. Some may be simple lies, but some are definitely pros at it.

Scammers create fake online profiles, often using photos stolen from other profiles. They take advantage of your vulnerability, loneliness, and empathy to try to steal from you.

My son had someone take his image and use it on a fake profile. A simple image search by copying an image and putting it in a search engine may bring up several names.

This is usually a sure-fire way to know the person you are dealing with is a scammer.

After a while, I started to see a pattern. Dating profiles quite often have similarities that stand out.

Read them carefully, don't just look at the title and good looking pictures. Quite often, the profile sounds just like the kind of guy you are looking for...think this is a coincidence?

They create profiles they know will attract the kind of woman that is vulnerable to their con. This is known as a "Romance Scam."

These are usually a group of men (quite often working out of countries such as Nigeria). If you read the profiles and messages carefully, you will see their mistakes, such as broken English, getting their stories mixed up, forgetting details of previous conversations, etc.

Here are a few things to watch out for to avoid being conned or catfished.

- They are very often widowers (this is because women are sensitive and feel empathy for a widowed man)
- They often say they are looking for marriage (again targeting lonely women wanting love)
- They tend to have certain occupations such as being in the military or a

profession like a surgeon, architect or engineer; they are often in the mining, gold, or petroleum industries.

- They use broken English...look for wording such as *"I will like to know you more"*
- These profiles often are up for a few days, then disappear, but miraculously they appear again in a very similar profile
- They may have a younger child who is away at school or something similar

About Barry

Hi there im barry , im a nice outstanding and loving man. I will love to find the woman of my dreams

Conversation Starters (i.e. what you'd like to do on a first date...)

Hi there i will love to talk about love, Chat with friends and meet someone special

jesse043

Hello, my name is Gilbert, am a resident of New York, Am an Engineer, into estate development also deal on germ stones. my friend told me about this site. Am looking for a serious relationship to a loving, understanding and caring lady.

Hello Gloria, How are you
doing? You have a nice profile
here and i will like to know
more about you. Greg

I am good thanks

nandocom60

My name is Anthony Miele ...I am not here for jokes or games and i am so serious
about my words .I am new to online dating, and i really don't know much about it...am
looking for a soul mate, best friend and lover who is interested in a long term
relationship

lovespinot

That's sounds good
Gloria

lovespinot

Don't you want to know about my book

nandocom60

i will love to know

johnnieq

You are welcome. Thanks for writing back. I must say you are such a beautiful woman and looking very attractive to me. I'm a gold and gemstones dealer and also an investor, i buy raw gold and gemstones from different part of the continent mostly in Brazil,Asia,Middle East and South America in large quantity and import them to the States to resell, mostly to the small scale dealers and also to those who refines but i have a dream lol. I want to meet a woman that's financially independent and secure just like I am coz I love my job and I'm independent. How long have you been in this dating site? And what has been your experience of online dating? David

baaad_boy

You're so beautiful that every man would want to hold hands with you someday. Looking into your Profile alone, shows me a beautiful world. And i guess i'll be the luckiest man getting to talk to you. If i were to present your picture in heaven, most of the Angels would hide their faces in shame... I'm Miller

comefishmeout06

Hi Gorgeous..... I am so sorry for the late response... I was so busy which is why i haven't got time to respond back yet.... Well i am ready to give it all to the woman that will love me for whom i am and not what i am, I am romantic man and also ready to pamper and spoil you if you would accept me..... all am asking for in return is walk by my side and hold my hands till the end of time, I can't for us to get along and also to start calling you my love... What do you think.

They profess strong feelings for you very early on in the relationship, often going overboard with words of love, how beautiful you are, how special, etc.

arosefl62

Merry Christmas

lovespinot

Same to you

arosefl62

I am sweet, caring and compassionate a true romantic,very casual, loyal, honest, friendly person, and value friendships. Have learned in my lifetime to depend on myself and sometimes that makes me very independent. I am looking for someone who will look at me for who I really am, kind and sensitive. Would like to meet someone that wants to be cared for and loved, who will be honest and committed in a relationship. Like music and so on, i will like to get to know about your likes too bye for now and please take good care

Maxwell

You may wonder why this one is here...I got that same message more than once...word for word...from other profiles with other pictures.

It is a perfect example of how they send out multiple messages, and often you are targeted with the same message or pretty darn close.

They try to get you to leave the site almost immediately by saying they are rarely on it and want to chat by phone, text or email

Ilovemylife101

I'm not always on here though

Ilovemylife101

Is it ok to have your phone number so we can have a better communication and get to meet at some point

lovespinot

I prefer to chat here

EasygoingCreativeFoodie

Hi Gloria, how are you doing? I hope you are enjoying your weekend. I wish you well with your company tournament next week. I enjoy cooking any kind of food. It would be nice to cook Tenderloin Steaks with Herb Cheese Topping, for you someday. You look great in your pic and have an interesting profile. I will be glad to get to know you better, will you mind emailing me via rw5174547@gmail.com so that we can get to know each other better as I don't come on this web site often. I guess that will be easier as well for further conversation if you feel comfortable with it and don't mind writing me an email. I will reply and tell you about myself. My regards, Robert

They say they live in a certain city, but if they give you their phone number the area code will not match the city, and if you question it they have some excuse ready, such as they are traveling at the moment

KevinJ5959

My number is 548 800 4064.

lovespinot

What country is it from

lovespinot

How is the weather in Nigeria

KevinJ5959

It's raining and cold
And you'll like it here 😀

Then sometimes, it is obvious they have not read the details of your profile or your answers.

In this example, the scammer is probably talking to several women at the same time; that is why he has asked the same question twice.

Also, he is probably talking to someone else on Match while talking to me and he is getting us mixed up.

magicmoments88

How long have you been on match

lovespinot

I'm not on match
Read my profile if you want to chat

magicmoments88

How is the search going?

lovespinot

have you even read my profile? you have asked me the same question twice, even though i have answered it
you thought i was on match when we are on pof
are you a scammer getting your targets mixed up

Then there is this new ploy, where they pretend they are setting you up with someone else.

Missycat6617

Good Evening Pretty,

How are you this evening i'm sorry if I do this to disturb you, If there is one person you need to meet on this is my my boss Karl, your profile is amazing, very honest,caring above all so sweet,that's a nice smile you put on, my boss saw your pictures on my profile and he caught interest in you, he is a busy man and he is not into Internet dating, he said you seem like a woman whom has found balance in all aspect of life is a hard thing to come by this days. age 59, Widower, a good listener,Good Looking , all round a complete gentle man, it might be worth it in the end. Take a chance and get to know him, by sending him email via: kawalter31@gmail.com take a chance and get to send him Email. wish you guys best of luck.

fortyfour

Hello, its a pleasure to let you know my commander John has not stopped talking about you. He can't join the site because he's still active in service and at the moment he doesn't have access to the site due to some restrictions so all i did was sent him your picture and he requested i send you a note so here i am doing just that. I was a chef in the scullery dept and I've been out of service due to health reasons and I don't also have a picture because my profile will not be active after 48 hours as i requested to take it down (Met someone already). John is handsome, has a good sense of humor, caring and he is divorced. I surely want him happy again now that he will be retired and back home full-time.

He's got a house in Ontario just few miles from you and that made me think you both would be a perfect match, John is all a woman would want in a man, I'll suggest that you give it a try because we can't predict how and when love can be found and literally sometimes it just needs a helping hand to find that special someone, If you'd like to know him send him a note: johnlovescardinal@gmail.com and he will share more about himself with you and pictures. Let him know where you live precisely in your email because he wouldn't communicate with anyone outside his region.

I wish you both luck.
Mcdowell

19

Working with the Fraud Squad

I was at work one day when I got a call. It was from a detective with the York Regional Fraud Squad. (York Region is an area in Southern Ontario just north of the city of Toronto). This was in 2014.

He asked me if I had been speaking with someone named *Ryan Hull* from the Plenty of Fish dating site. I answered, *"Not to my knowledge."*

He then told me that my name had come up quite a few times during an investigation into a Romance Scam.

Actually, he meant my profile name, and of course, he was able to find my real name and contact information as part of his investigation.

He told me details about this man called *"Ryan"* and described some of our conversations that he had discovered on the dating site. He also said he found phone records indicating that the man had several conversations with me.

When I went home that night, I went to my personal email and went back a few months, as that is when the detective told me these conversations took place.

I found quite a few emails between this person and myself, including his picture.

As I read these emails, I started to remember this man. I recalled that I was suspicious of him for many reasons.

However, when we first started talking, I had not yet had any reason to doubt him, so that is why I allowed him to email me.

We started out chatting on the dating site. Then he told me that he wasn't on the site that often as he traveled quite a bit for business and that it would be much easier if we could chat by email.

I now know that this is just one of the tricks these cons use. They try to get you off the dating site as quickly as possible, but I did not know this at that time.

Fortunately, I had kept these emails, and not only did they serve to refresh my memory, but I was able to pass them along to the police and they became part of the investigation.

It was quite a while ago, so I do not remember everything, but this man said a lot of things in these emails that raised my suspicions.

He traveled a lot, and he actually sent me a gift, touristy souvenir stuff. It wasn't much, just enough to make me believe he was actually in Ireland.

He told me he was in the process of selling a business and starting a new one. He also called me several times, supposedly from China, where the sale of his business was occurring.

The calls came from a number that when I googled showed that the area code was from China.

I was later told by the detective that groups of criminals worked together as a team and that several different men could be pretending to be *Ryan*.

The gifts and phone calls were to lend authenticity to their claims of being out of the country.

I was also told they have the means to reroute phone calls so that they appear to be coming from another country.

There were several things that made me wonder about him, but the real clincher for me was elaborate details he went into about the sale of his business; how lucrative it was, how he would be set for life financially and would be able to stop traveling and finally get to meet and have a serious, loving relationship with me.

In fact, he emailed me a copy of his contract.

By now, I pretty much figured he was trying to con me, but call it curiosity or just wanting to know that I was right, so I led him to believe that I believed.

After all, who in their right mind would send a copy of a contract, a lucrative one with all the details, to a woman they have never met?

Who would make several long-distance phone calls, from China to a woman they have yet to meet. Especially while they were in the middle of negotiating a big contract?

You see, these guys are so used to conning naive, lonely and desperate women, they had no idea they were actually dealing with a woman that had been through that experience before and therefore knew the signs to look out for.

Although my previous experience being conned was very different. With Andrew, I actually knew the man, dated the man, and thought I was in love with and engaged to the man.

This was totally different as I had only talked with him on the site, by email, and by phone.

But my years of experience on these dating sites, talking to other obvious con men, as well as doing my own research, gave me the heads up I needed to protect myself from ever being conned again!

Later, a few months after I had helped the detectives with their investigation, I was contacted by the media relations coordinator.

She told me they were putting together a video to warn women of the dangers of online dating and Romance Scams. She asked if I had any interest in being a part of it.

I jumped at the opportunity to help other women to avoid being conned, and to advise them of the signs to look out for.

For me making this video, as well as finally publishing this book has been very cathartic.

Please watch this video and pass it along to anyone and everyone that you think can benefit from it.

As this *Ryan* guy never did get to con me, most of my story was about my experience with Andrew and online dating in general.

They have taped us in the dark as to protect our privacy. I am "Joan."

https://www.youtube.com/watch?v=peb10yVpA2w

York Region Police warning of increased dangers of online ...
https://globalnews.ca › video › york-region-police-warning-of-increased-dan...

Jun 16, 2015
The 'bad guys' have evolved: OPP issue online fraud warning ahead of ...
York Regional Police release ...
Missing: ~~squad~~ | Must include: squad

More stories below ▼

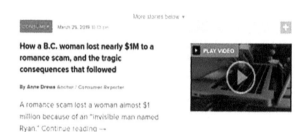

CONSUMER   March 29, 2019 10:13 pm

**How a B.C. woman lost nearly $1M to a
romance scam, and the tragic
consequences that followed**

By Anne Drews Anchor / Consumer Reporter

A romance scam lost a woman almost $1
million because of an "invisible man named
Ryan." Continue reading →

**There were two other women that made this
video as well. I never met either one of them,
but from what I understand, they were even
more unfortunate than me.**

MEDIA RELEASE
CHARGES LAID IN 1.5 MILLION DOLLAR ROMANCE FRAUD

The York Regional Police Major Fraud Unit has laid over 40 charges against nine people in connection with a romance fraud where seven victims have lost $1.5 million. Investigators believe there are more victims and are asking them to come forward.

The Major Fraud Unit began an investigation in July 2014, after a woman came forward to report that she had been a victim of a fraud. Police discovered that a group of individuals from the Toronto area had been operating an organized, criminal network, targeting woman on dating websites.

In this type of fraud, the suspect creates a false dating profile and goes to great lengths to makes this false identity believable. The suspect will use a number of tactics and schemes to build trust and establish a relationship with the victim. These relationships often progress very quickly to an emotional point where the victim is so invested in the relationship that they feel compelled to help when the suspect begins to ask for money.

As the investigation continued, six additional victims were identified who had similar experiences and a variety of financial losses, as well as a very large number of woman who the suspects attempted to get money from but were unsuccessful. In this investigation the suspects were operating on various dating websites using the names Benjamin D. **BAKER** and Ryan **HULL**. Nine suspects have been arrested and charged and this investigation is ongoing.

https://www.yorkregion.com/news-story/9291603-romance-scam-romeo-no-prince-charming-for-richmond-hill-victim/

20

Then there was Julio's Gallo's Son!

I was quickly becoming a pro at spotting these spineless, scum-sucking bottom dwellers, so I felt sure I would never be had again. It was getting to the point where I could almost point out a profile and say with utter confidence *"that's one of them!"*

Then I met Robert. He sent me a message and seemed believable enough, but he did not have a picture.

After chatting for a bit, I asked if I could see his picture. I did not want to waste his or my time if he looked like a troll.

He gave me a story about not wanting to upload it as he didn't want people he worked with to recognize him.

I have talked to several men that have told me the same thing, and for the most part, that is a good reason.

Some people are embarrassed and don't want friends or co-workers to know their business, and to see them on a dating site.

In fact, I occasionally see someone I know personally on these sites. I actually found a co-worker on the same site as me.

I didn't even know he was separated, and we sent a few joke messages back and forth, then had a good laugh over it at the office the next day.

Another time I was talking to a man that told me if I saw his picture, I would recognize him as he had recently been in our federal election running for a local seat.

When I tried to guess who that might be, based on his profile description, he ghosted me and disappeared.

Back to Robert. He said I could see his picture if I went to the E & J Gallo Wine website. At the time, there was a picture of the family on the site. He told me he was Robert Gallo, Julio's son, and pointed out which one he was.

I said to him, "Are you telling me you are Julio Gallo's son??? THE JULIO GALLO? As in the billionaire wine family?"

He answered, yes. Well, my "Spidey senses" were really clicking in. There was no way in hell he was from that rich family and on a dating site and talking to ME!

I just knew I was talking to another con artist. But my curiosity was raised, and I just had to see how far he would carry this. So we talked for a bit, and he asked me a lot of questions about myself.

I was convinced he was a scammer. One of the things they do is ask a lot of questions about you so they can determine if you are a candidate to be conned.

They want to get a feel for how vulnerable you are; how much money they might be able to get out of you.

But I played along and led him to think I was very well off and lonely and to give the impression I was an easy target.

As we chatted, he told me he left the family business and was now living and working in Canada, in a suburb that is known for its wealthy residents.

He told me that he was a land developer and was a partner with his two sons-in-law in their home building firm. He gave me the name of the company.

He asked me to meet him for a drink, which kind of threw me for a loop, as most of the cons I am targeted by never actually intend to meet you.

Most of them try to find ways to not meet with you by always being out of the country, traveling for business, or some such story.

They usually try to build a relationship with you away from the dating site, by email or texting or phone calls.

The reason for not meeting you is that they are usually from Nigeria or some other part of the world.

I agreed to meet him for a drink at a bar near the airport. He didn't look exactly like the picture on the Gallo website, but he told me it was quite old, which made sense. He did sort of look like that guy.

We had a glass of wine, and I had a nice time. I was still very wary, but he seemed quite knowledgeable about the area of the city he told me he lived in, the construction industry, wine production and anything else we chatted about.

I had gone to this date with some research under my belt, determined to catch him in a lie.

I had read some about the Gallo family history, memorized some of the names of Julio and Ernest's children and grandchildren and some of the history and tragedy the family had experienced.

This guy was good. He knew the names, positions at the winery, family history. Heck, I could not catch him in a lie.

Could he be for real?? I still had my doubts. Further research was needed.

He had mentioned the address where he lived. He had also given me his cell phone number.

I called the number but got a voice mail message intended for construction workers looking for a job. I googled the phone number and found a job placement ad for general labour and other home building trades.

I researched the company that he said he was partnered in. According to the website, the company was founded and owned by two brothers.

So far, it seemed like he might be telling me the truth!

So now, I was confused.

I decided to drive by the address he mentioned was his home. It was a huge, beautiful estate home on the lake just south of Toronto.

I called a realtor friend of mine and asked him if he could find out the name of the person that owned the home. He called me back and gave me a woman's name.

I guess it was possible that he was renting the home from her, but that did not seem to make sense to me...not if he was a partner in a firm that built luxury homes.

I called him and suggested we meet again. This time I was determined to solve this puzzle.

Well, he could have fooled me again.

He was charming, and I left still not knowing what to think. I could not catch him in a lie without letting on that I suspected him, so I figured it was time to ask the Pros.

I called my contact at York Regional and told them my suspicions and suggested they look into it. But, as he had not committed any crime, their hands were tied. They did think he seemed "off," but there was nothing they could do.

But I would not leave it at that. I contacted the Home Building firm and told the receptionist what I thought.

She put me through to their lawyer. I told the lawyer what I knew. She told me that the company was owned by two brothers, but they did not have a father-in-law that was part of the firm and had never heard of Robert Gallo.

At least they were warned that someone was going around pretending to be part of their company.

I guess I will never know the truth about who he is, but my gut is telling me he was a liar.

He may not have had any intention of conning me; he may have just been trying to impress me, either way, you can bet I blocked his phone number and profile from my dating site.

21

Don't Just Take My Word for It

In my present occupation as a Marketing Manager, I write a lot of copy, and I do a lot of research.

I want to use those skills to help you understand how these guys think and operate so you will not have to suffer the same pain I have experienced.

There is a lot of information out there; I don't expect you to believe everything I say.

Please see below some references to check out and some articles I have found. These have been cut and pasted as I found them and are not my words.

https://www.consumerreports.org/dating-relationships/online-dating-romance-scams/#social_fb_comments

It Pays to Be Paranoid

The CR survey found that 35 percent of respondents who've tried online dating felt they had been grossly misled by someone's online profile, and 12 percent said they'd been scammed. Experts say online daters are always wise to be skeptical regarding what someone they've met online, and not in the flesh, tells them.

Most dating websites—even ones that cost money—don't vet the people who sign up. So it's up to you to determine how truthful a person is being in his or her profile.   To recognize and avoid romance scams, follow these tips.

Run a search.

Copy the images your online correspondent has posted to his or her profile, then run them through a reverse-image search engine, such as TinEye or Google Images. If the images come up associated with a person who has another name or lives in a different city, you have good reason to suspect they were stolen from someone else's profile.

Interrogate the backstory.

A little online stalking can go a long way. Type the name of the person you met online into Google or Bing and see what comes up.

You might not be able to surface information like criminal records, but from their social media profiles, LinkedIn page, and other information you find, you should be able to get a sense of whether what they are telling you comports with the facts.

According to the FBI, romance scams and similar confidence scams cost consumers more money than any other kind of Internet fraud. In 2016, the last year for which data is available, consumers lost more than $230 million this way.

The FBI says it may be embarrassing for victims to report this type of fraud scheme because of the personal relationships that are developed, so the real numbers are probably higher.

As one result, fear of a horrible first date is just one of the things a would-be online dater has to worry about.

According to a recent Consumer Reports Online Dating Survey of more than 114,000 subscribers, among the respondents who were considering online dating but were hesitant, 46 percent said they were concerned about being scammed.

Their worry is not overstated. Romance scams really can happen to anyone.

"Most people think the victims are middle-aged women who can't get a date, but I have worked with men and women of all ages—doctors and lawyers, CEOs of companies, people from the entertainment industry—who you'd never think in a million years would fall for these scams but do," says Barb Sluppick, who runs Romance Scams, a watchdog site, and online support group.

"Typically the scammer builds trust by writing long letters over weeks or months and crafting a whole persona for their victims," says David Farquhar, Supervisory Special Agent with the FBI. "That big investment gives victims a false sense that the relationship must be real."

Eventually, a pitch for money comes. Often the scammer will say an emergency situation has arisen and money is needed fast to avoid dire consequences.

This makes it hard for the victim to do due diligence. The scammer might say that an immediate family member has a medical emergency and needs money for treatment, or that he has been wrongly arrested and needs help with bail money and legal support.

"There was one woman who got scammed for over a million dollars, her whole retirement nest egg," Farquhar says.

22

The Biggest Scam of All

I no longer had any confidence that I was going to find my MR. RIGHT on dating sites.

During the years, I had tried them all; Plenty of Fish, Match, EHarmony, Mate, OK Cupid, Zoosk, SeniorPeopleMeet, Our Time, SilverSingles, Elite Singles, Tinder, Fitness Singles and Millionaire Match; and those are just the ones I remember.

I can't even begin to imagine the time and money I have invested looking for a life partner.

I thought the ones where I paid a subscription fee might be more fruitful, thinking that if the men are paying to meet women, they might truly be looking for a relationship...NO.

I reasoned that if I joined a site where everyone paid, and someone else matched us based on metrics, and not just looks, that might work...NO.

I did not have the patience to wait for weeks to see if someone I was matched with would send me a message or respond to a message I sent them. This is not my style.

I thought maybe the dating sites that appealed to older, mature adults might work...NO.

I thought the ones that promised love and criminal checks might work...NO.

Maybe one that appealed to career-oriented people...NO.

Ok, what about finding a guy that liked that I golfed...NO.

Maybe I could meet a man that had money and wasn't a loser on the Millionaire site...NO.

I went through a bad period where I thought, ok, if I can't find a man for a real, loving, serious relationship, maybe I would settle for a fling; fun, sex, FWB, hence Tinder and others.

I hate to admit it, but I even joined some Cougar site for a while. It was good for my ego, having good looking, younger men wanting to be with me. It made me feel young, sexy, and desirable.

Until I started getting messages from men so young, it made me feel stupid and desperate. That left a bad taste in my mouth.

I have met the most men through Plenty of Fish. Lots of cons there, that's for sure. There are also a lot of younger guys looking to learn from a mature woman.

But I liked that I had the option to search through profiles of men; in other words, I could search for the criteria that appealed to me, such as age, race, height, weight, income, interests, occupation, etc.

I tried paying for the upgraded membership, hoped that might get the better, more serious candidates...NO.

Now don't get me wrong. Over the years, I have talked to many nice men from many dating sites. They just didn't appeal to me for a variety of reasons.

Maybe I did not find them attractive or feel we had much in common, or they lived too far away.

They might not have been in my income level, meaning they could probably not afford the kind of lifestyle that I like with dining out, golf and travel. Or they may not have had the same education or level of intelligence.

They may have been too young or old for me or had children living at home.

We may have been at different stages in our lives. When I was in my late 50's and early 60's retirement was not on my horizon, or being a grandmother, so often men at that stage of their life did not appeal to me.

I usually prefer dating men about ten years younger than me, as I feel we have more in common such as careers, activities, etc.

The problem with that is they often have younger children, still living at home, especially if they had them later in their life. I am not interested in being a stepmother again.

Been there, done that.

As we age, we get more set in our ways and particular about what we want. I was becoming less willing to settle for anything less, but yet, I still yearned to find a suitable man to spend my life with...to enjoy my life with.

I no longer needed a man to take care of me, but I still wanted a partner.

So I decided to try something totally different.

I had seen commercials on television for a company called Life Mates. I often wondered what they did differently from online dating sites, so I finally gave in and called and set up an appointment.

They were a matchmaking service. Unlike online dating sites, they actually took the time to sit with you and interview you.

They had me fill out all kinds of paperwork and questionnaires, with the goal being to match me with the most suitable candidates.

They also said they did security and criminal checks on all of their members. I thought this would be a great way to find someone that was not a lying, cheating, married SOB.

I would also be assured that these men had well-paying jobs or at least the means to pay for this service. You see it wasn't cheap...it cost me close to $3,000 dollars for their services and I was told that men paid even more!

They even sent me to a professional photographer for model quality photos that were touched up.

Now, I don't understand why they did this, as I later learned that we never got to see the images of our matches, so these men I was being matched with never got a chance to see these wonderful photos.

I expect now it was just a way for them to justify the outrageous fees they charged.

However, I did not know that at the time, and I left with a new enthusiasm that these professional matchmakers could find me my MR. RIGHT.

Over the next two years, they introduced me to a grand total of eight men. Not one of which was even remotely suitable.

After each meeting, I would tell them what I did and did not like so they could refine their matches.

I agreed to meet all of the suggested matches because there were so few, and I had paid so much money for this service.

After two years of telling them how unsatisfied I was with their matching, they went out of business.

I wonder why?

23

A is for Attitude – O is for Opportunity

At this point, not much was working for me, not on the dating sites, and not with a matchmaking service.

I had lost my confidence, what little I had. My attitude sucked. I found this was spilling over into all my life, including my career.

So it was time to make a change. This time, not to my looks, but to my attitude.

I started reading some motivational and self-help type books; Dating relationship books; How to Get a Man, How to Keep a Man, How to Love Yourself, etc.

I realized that although a lot of the guys I had talked to and met may have been liars, cheaters, scammers, and losers...I knew that some of them were probably ok guys that I didn't give a chance.

My suspicions may have caused me to overlook some quality men.

Maybe they were not the problem, maybe I was?

You see, I was so intent, so wrapped up in finding a suitable, lifelong mate that I was putting out the wrong vibe. I was scaring guys away. Guess that's why so many ghosts??

So I took a break from dating sites for a while and decided to work on me.

I decided I needed to find hobbies, make friends, and find other things to enjoy in my life. Instead of concentrating all of my efforts on finding love, I needed to find happiness and joy.

I am very fortunate to have a large, supportive, loving family. I have six sisters, and most of us work together for the same company. We also like to do a lot of things together socially.

We started to travel together over the last few years. We even named our little group, *"The Travelling Ladies."* This group also included my brother's wife and a couple of girlfriends from work.

Previously I had only traveled to places like Florida, Mexico, and the Dominican Republic. It was the kind of holiday that worked best with a husband or for a family vacation.

But the ladies started to travel to Europe. I found a new passion that included cruising, seeing wonderful sights, experiencing different cultures, trying new foods, and of course, tasting and appreciating wonderful wines.

I have been on several cruises, as well as land trips to Italy, France, Spain, Greece, Malta, Croatia, England, and there are many other places on my bucket list I want to see.

The times I have traveled with the ladies have been some of the most enjoyable of my life. There is nothing like a group of ladies to make you laugh till you pee your pants.

My father had always suggested to me "*make some girlfriends*," and I had finally decided to heed his advice.

These ladies, mostly sisters, are my best friends. I can share anything and everything with them. They are there for me during good times and bad.

I also found that once my attitude changed, my relationships with my friends from high school improved.

With my new and improved attitude, I no longer felt intimidated or insecure. I realized they accepted me as I am; they always had.

Another change I made was to join a bowling league. I had always enjoyed bowling and was in a league with my late husband when we were younger.

I found a group to join, and although I did not meet any men to date and did not make any girlfriends, the people were nice, and I was putting myself out there.

Rather than spending all my time looking at a screen and trying to find a guy, now I was getting exercise and having a social life.

I also decided to take up golf. I had golfed over the years with both husbands, but never took it up seriously.

I decided it would be a good way to make some friends, get some exercise, and it is also a good way to network professionally.

So I bought a new set of clubs, golf clothes, and all the stuff needed, and I joined a local ladies league and started to golf once a week after work.

It was hard for me to do, as I have never really been a joiner. Although I can be very extroverted and friendly, it does take me a while to become comfortable in a new environment; and I had never been particularly good at sports.

A lot of my family golf, and a lot of my peers at work, suppliers, etc. golf. Our company has a fundraising golf tournament each year, and I had the opportunity to participate.

I did not want to embarrass myself, so I took some lessons, and slowly I am improving, and my confidence is growing. Now I enjoy going to the driving range on most weekends.

24

Taking Care of Business

At work, an opportunity arose.

Our VP of Marketing was getting close to retirement age, and I knew they were going to need someone that could take on some of his duties.

I realized that if I worked hard, put in a real effort, and showed them what I was capable of, there could be a good opportunity for me to advance my career.

**But to do this, I needed to show them
my new and improved attitude.**

This was good for me for a lot of reasons.

My career was not where I wanted it to be. I was not enjoying my work, but this opportunity that had become available was my chance to show everyone, my family, my friends, my coworkers, but mostly myself, just what I was capable of.

You see, I had always loved business, marketing in particular. I took Marketing in college and had many good jobs in both sales and marketing. I have always been ambitious.

At one time, my late husband and I had a small marketing company, but hard times and a minor recession caused us to lose our business.

We had lost everything; our home, our cars, our credit. We had to declare bankruptcy and this all happened when my son was just a baby.

We had several hard years, and some of this led to my husband's eventual passing.

Between the bankruptcy, my husband's illness, our moving out of the city, and my need to raise my son alone, I had to put my career aspirations on hold.

This opportunity was a chance for me to change all that.

To get back into the kind of work I loved. To be challenged and to use my creative and intellectual abilities to not only help myself, but the company my family and I are a part of.

My career has flourished. I became a supervisor, then the Marketing Manager. I was finally doing the work I loved and feeling confident, important, needed, and respected.

My son was proud of me, my family was proud of me, but most importantly, I was proud of me.

25

#SixtyThreeistheNewMe

So now, my career was satisfying. Who said you had to be young to move up the corporate ladder and make a name for yourself.

I was making new friends. I was traveling, golfing, bowling, and generally getting out there. These are things I did not do, could not afford to do when I was younger and had a small child to raise alone.

But still, I was missing something. Although much happier than I had been in quite a while, I still went through periods of sadness and loneliness. I still longed for a life-partner.

I had my friends over for a dinner party one night, and my late girlfriend's husband and I were swapping tales of our dating woes, as he has also tried online dating.

I mentioned that in all the years since my late husband passed, no one had ever introduced me to a man. There had been no dinner party invites or blind date setups for me.

I always thought that would be the best way to meet a good guy, someone real; if your friends knew and liked him, he had to be ok.

Two weeks later, one of my girlfriends called me and told me she had been thinking over what I said, and she realized her and her husband knew a guy that might be right for me.

So they set us up.

His name was Ted. He was a few years younger than me.

On our first date, he took me out for dinner. He was nice looking, had a good job, home, all that. He lived in the same neighbourhood as my friends.

He was divorced and had daughters around my son's age. We seemed to have a fair bit in common, so we started dating.

At first, it was a lot of fun. We met in the summer, so we went wine tasting, out for dinners, went on a harbor cruise.

He met my son, my family, and my friends. We played cards with my sisters and their husbands, and he came to Christmas dinner with my family.

By now, we had been seeing each other for about six months. I liked Ted and thought that we had a future together. However, he still had not introduced me to his family and friends.

I tried to be patient and understanding. It seemed like he liked me, so I thought if I gave it time, Ted would eventually come around and introduce me to his daughters.

But the months went by, and we fell into a routine. Ted would come to my place, and we would have dinner, watch a movie, play some backgammon and go to bed. In the morning, I would make us breakfast and by noon, he would have left.

I usually did the cooking. Ted did help with the clean up a bit. Occasionally, when his daughter was away, I would be invited to his place, then he would do the cooking.

We occasionally entertained the couple that introduced us, but other than that, it was only my family that we socialized with.

He was not much into wine or drinking for that matter, so eventually, he stopped bringing over wine, and I bought my own.

Once when I hinted that I would like to go out for dinner, he reluctantly agreed, however when it came time to pay the bill, Ted looked at me and said: "*dinner out was your idea; maybe you should open your wallet once in a while.*"

I looked at him and said, *"I open my wallet every weekend when I buy and make you dinner and breakfast."*

Slowly things started to cool between us. The sex that was so passionate and exciting started to become boring and feel forced.

I worried that I would never meet his girls and that the future I had dreamt was possible, was not going to happen.

Ted was not much interested in travel. He was very content just to spend quiet evenings at home. Now I am not a *"party girl,"* but I did like to get out every once in a while.

I went on a trip to Europe with the ladies in June, 11 months after having met Ted. While I was gone, I sent him several emails with pictures from my travels, but I never got a response back.

When I got home from my vacation, I was looking forward to seeing him, but he did not seem anxious to see me. Or in a hurry.

When we did get together, he did not have much enthusiasm for hearing about my adventures or seeing my pictures.

The only enthusiasm I saw was to get into the bedroom!

That's when I realized nothing was going to change. It was time to give it up and move on. So I broke up our relationship.

I have since tried to stay friends, but he does not seem to be interested in that.

26

Back to the Drawing Board

I am sure by now that many of you wonder, "what now"?

I sure do.

As you can see, I have tried everything I can to meet men; dating websites, matchmaking service, joining clubs and taking up sports, going to singles dances, and meetups.

I took up bowling and golf, and although I enjoy them, I have not met one man through those endeavors.

I have not met any through networking and career.

So yes, I am back on the dating websites. It seems to be the only way to meet men these days.

I will date a man for friendship and companionship, and sometimes just to get out there and have an enjoyable evening.

And I will give a man a chance, as I have learned that you cannot always judge a book by its cover.

But I am not the same woman I was. I have grown and experienced so much. I now go to dating sites with new confidence.

I have learned that to find love; I must first love myself. I accept myself the way I am; weight, age, wrinkles. I own it all.

I understand that I deserve and am worthy of love.

I now look for quality, instead of quantity. A quality man can sense the confidence, intelligence, and attitude I bring to the table, and they find that appealing in a woman.

Yes, I still get messages from the con artists, sex nuts, young guys, and losers. But, I am a little more cautious, more aware of what I do and don't want. My criteria are set pretty high, and I am not willing to settle for less.

Dating sites can be very addictive. There is a certain freedom to be who you want, to say what you want. You can be someone totally different than who you normally are. You can search for specific types of men or relationships.

You can experiment and try things you might never have otherwise done. You can expand your horizons and meet people you might never have met.

You can find friends, lovers, and maybe, just maybe, if your attitude is good, and you have some luck, you might find love.

I am a hopeful romantic, ever an optimist. My glass may get empty, but it is always half full.

Who the heck is gloriaM?

gloriaM is my brand. I am a single mother, aged 63, at the time this book was published. I have a grown son, a large, close-knit family, and a great job.

I am a Marketing Manager for a large advertising company in Toronto. I am passionate about business, writing and designing compelling marketing materials.

I love my job as it lets me look at pretty pictures all day and research topics of interest, as I make beautiful wall calendars.

I love wine, travel, golf, backgammon, and spending time with family. I am an avid reader, and now an author. Thanks to Covid 19 I just finished writing my second book, an erotic suspense thriller.

I have created an author website and blog at **gloriamoodie.com**

Here you will see beautiful imagery and read about the topics that interest me such as wonderful places to travel, great wines to try, helpful tips on mindfulness and living healthy and motivational and inspirational messages.

It is also a place where we can share our stories and help each other navigate the world of online dating and looking for love.

Please write to me at

gloriamoodie@hotmail.com

And YES, guys, I am still a great catch!

Now for an excerpt from my next book, a psychological suspense thriller all about online dating and murder

An Innocent Addiction

Prologue

Ashley liked sex; in fact, she loved sex. She loved the way it made her feel; sexy, desirable, wanted. Powerful and in control!

Ashley craved the attention. She was drawn to the excitement that a little bit of danger brought, after all, it was her business what she did and with whom.

Ashley's growing addiction to online dating provided her with the means and opportunity to satisfy those needs.

She wasn't hurting anyone...and that's what she thought right up until the moment someone was killed.

Neil is obsessed with Ashley. If only his wife did not get in the way. He cyberstalks her when she refuses to see him anymore, saying she would not date a married man. But he must have her.

Neil must find a way to become single. Divorce is not an option.

But Ashley must never learn what Neil is willing to do to make that happen.

But Ashley has changed. She now realizes the power she craves comes from another source. She is determined to catch not only Neil but all those that take advantage of women and their love and trust.

Ashley is determined to catch Neil, and beat him at his game, or die doing so.

CPSIA information can be obtained
at www.ICGtesting.com
Printed in the USA
LVHW071541180920
666492LV00013B/775